P9-DEL-752

WOLVES

S E Y M O U R S I M O N

Updated Edition

 Smithsonian |  Collins

An Imprint of HarperCollinsPublishers

Imagine snow falling silently in the great woodlands of North America. The only sounds are from the trees creaking and tossing in the wind. Suddenly the quiet is broken by the eerie howling of a wolf. And all the frightening stories and legends that you've heard about the treacherous and sly wolf and the evil werewolf begin to race through your mind.

But what is this animal of our imagination truly like? Are wolves savage and destructive hunters of people and livestock? Or are they one of nature's most misunderstood creatures? It is possible that people don't like wolves because they don't know very much about them. For example, there is no record of a healthy wolf ever trying to kill a human in North America. Perhaps by learning about the wolf and how it lives in the natural world, we can begin to tell the difference between the real animal and the fables we've created.

In many ways, wolves are like dogs and lions, yet wolves have a bad reputation, unlike dogs and lions. Dogs are our "best friends," but all the dogs in the world are descended from wolves that were domesticated more than ten thousand years ago. And most of the things people like about dogs are also true about wolves.

Like dogs, wolves are very loyal to other wolves in their family. Wolves raised by people become loyal to those people as well. Dogs are friendly and intelligent, and these traits are also found in wolves. Wolves in a pack are playful with one another. They are among the most intelligent animals in nature.

Like lions, wolves are marvelous hunters that work in groups to catch their prey. Yet lions are called the "kings of the jungle," while wolves are described in many nursery tales as "sly and cowardly." It seems strange that people love dogs and admire lions but dislike wolves.

Wolves, like humans, are very adaptable to different climates and surroundings. At one time, wolves roamed across nearly all of North America, Europe, and Asia. Wolves can live in forests, grasslands, mountains, and swamps, and even in the frozen, treeless tundras of the north. Wolves can also eat almost anything they catch, from a moose to a mouse.

Wolves may look very different from one another. A wolf might be almost any color, from white to black, through shades and mixtures of cream, gray, brown, and red. Some wolves are heavily furred all over their bodies; others have more fur around their necks and backs. Some are large and powerful; others are smaller and quicker. Wolves even have different personalities; some are leaders, others are very social, and still others are "lone wolves."

Wolves may look and act differently from one another, but most wolves belong to the same species, called *Canis lupus* (*Canis* means "dog" and *lupus* means "wolf"). The wolf's closest relatives are the domestic dog, the coyote, jackals, and a dog of Australia called the dingo.

There are many subspecies of North American wolves and also lots of common names for the same kind of wolf. These include tundra (or arctic) wolves and gray (or timber) wolves, and lots of location names for wolves, such as the Mexican wolf, the Rocky Mountain wolf, the eastern timber wolf (shown here), the Texas gray wolf, and the Great Plains wolf (also called the lobo wolf or hunter). In colder locations, wolves usually have longer and thicker coats, smaller ears, and wider muzzles than wolves that live in warmer regions.

Hybrids (mixtures) such as wolf-dogs or wolf-coyotes are not really wolves at all. Even though wolf-dogs may look much like dogs, they are very difficult to train and can be dangerous if kept as pets in homes with small children.

The red wolf, *Canis rufus* (*rufus* means "red"), once numbered in the thousands and roamed all over the southeastern United States. But by the 1970s, there were fewer than one hundred left. Biologists captured every one they could find in Texas and Louisiana and bred them carefully, so that the pups were as much like the original red wolf as possible.

In 1987, eight red wolves were released in North Carolina's Alligator River National Wildlife Refuge. There they have produced a number of litters. When wolves are set free, they wear collars with radio tracking devices, so any that stray onto private lands can be found and retrieved. Breeding pairs have also been released onto four islands off the southeastern coast of the United States.

Some scientists think that the red wolf is really a hybrid, a mixture of the wolf and the coyote. But there are no coyotes or gray wolves living in nature near the reds, so any interbreeding has stopped.

Wolves can run for miles without tiring when they are hunting moose, elk, or other large prey. Wolves have strong muscles, and their legs are long and almost spindly. Like dogs, and most other animals, wolves run on their toes. This makes their legs even longer and lets them take long steps, so that they can run fast. Wolves seem to glide effortlessly when they run, almost like the shadow of a cloud drifting along the ground.

Wolves are the largest members of the dog family, bigger than any wild dogs and most domestic dogs. The wolf looks much like a German shepherd with thick, shaggy fur and a bushy tail. The fur is extra thick in winter and is a good protection against rain or snow. Water runs off a wolf's fur the way it runs off a raincoat.

An adult wolf can weigh from 40 to 175 pounds (18 to 80 kilograms) and stretch more than 6 feet (2 meters) from the tip of its nose to the end of its tail. Male wolves are usually larger than female wolves.

Like lions' and tigers' teeth, wolves' teeth are well suited for catching and eating other animals. Wolves have powerful jaws. The long, pointed teeth in the front sides of a wolf's jaws are called canines (KAY-nines). They are useful for grabbing and holding prey such as moose. The small teeth in the front between the canines are incisors (in-SIGH-zors), useful for picking meat off bones. Two teeth along both sides of the jaws are carnassials (car-NA-see-uls). They work like scissors to slice food into pieces small enough to be swallowed.

Wolves have marvelous hearing. They can hear other wolves howling from three or four miles away. They can locate mice by the squeals they make even when the rodents are beneath a snow-pack. Like bats and dolphins, wolves can also hear high-pitched sounds well above the range of human hearing. Wolves turn their ears from side to side. The direction the ears are pointing when the sound is loudest helps the wolf determine where the sound is coming from. Scientists believe that wolves hunt small prey more by sound than by smell or sight. Larger prey is often found by scent or by chance encounters.

Wolves live in packs, but that is just a name for a family of wolves. Packs are usually made up of a leader male and female wolf and their young along with some close relatives. An average wolf pack has five to eight wolves, but packs can have as few as two or three, or as many as twenty-five wolves.

The members of a pack are usually very friendly with one another. They hunt, travel, eat, and make noises together. Wolves bring bits of food to one another. They babysit one another's litters. They run around and play tag with one another and with the pups. They startle one another by hiding and then jumping out.

Wolves make all kinds of sounds besides howling; they bark, growl, whine, and squeak. Barking seems to be a warning when a wolf is surprised at its den. Growling is common among pups when they play, and adults growl when challenged by another wolf. Whines and squeaks are connected with playing, feeding, and general good feelings. Mothers squeak when the pups play too roughly; fathers squeak to call their pups.

Of all the sounds a wolf makes, its howl is the most familiar. A wolf howls by pointing its nose to the sky and then giving voice to a single high-pitched sound that rises sharply and then slides down in rippling waves. Wolves do not have to stand to howl; they can howl sitting or even lying on the ground. A wolf howls by itself or in groups of twos or threes. Often, other members of the pack join the chorus until the entire pack is howling.

Wolves howl at any time of day or night. Wolves howl to call the pack together before or after a hunt. They howl to locate one another when they are separated after a snowstorm or when in unfamiliar territory. They may howl to warn other wolf packs to stay away from their hunting grounds. And wolves even seem to howl just for the pleasure of it.

Howling increases seasonally during the winter months, and the sound may carry for six or more miles in cold, clear air. It's easy to see why people might have thought that the wolves were right at their doors when they heard the howling echoing across a shadowy moonlit snowscape.

Each wolf pack has a specific hierarchy. The leaders of a wolf pack are called the "alpha" male and the "alpha" female. They are usually the largest and strongest wolves in the pack, but packs may be as different from one another as individual wolves are different. A typical pack has an alpha male and an alpha female at the top, a lesser male and female in the middle called "beta" wolves, and less powerful wolves and pups at the bottom. (Alpha and beta are the letters A and B in the Greek alphabet.) Every member of a pack has a place or rank. Some wolves are higher and some are lower. This "dominance order" helps prevent fighting within the pack.

When two wolves in a pack have an argument, they may stick their ears and tails straight up, bare their teeth, and snarl at each other. Both wolves look fierce and ready to tear each other apart. But most times a wolf of a lower rank will give up before a fight starts with a wolf of a higher rank. To show that it has given up, the submissive wolf will lower its position or roll over on its back, flattening its ears and putting its tail between its legs. This behavior seems to prevent the dominant wolf from biting, so fights between pack members are usually settled without serious injuries.

Wolves hunt animals in different ways. A single wolf will hunt by itself for small prey, including mice, rabbits, squirrels, beavers, ducks, geese, and even fish when available. But much of their prey is large animals such as deer, elk, moose, caribou, musk oxen, and bighorn sheep. Most of these are hard to catch and can be dangerous when cornered, so wolves hunt them in packs.

One of the wolf's main prey is the moose. An adult moose may weigh over 1,000 pounds (450 kilograms) and stand over 6 feet (2 meters) tall at the shoulders. It has hooves that can injure and even kill a wolf. It is also strong and a good runner. So it is not surprising that roughly nine out of ten moose that wolves chase get away.

Wolves hunt moose by trying to encircle them and bring them to a standstill. One wolf may tear at the nose or the head of the moose while the others rip at the sides or the stomach. After wolves kill a large animal, they may rest a brief time or eat right away. Each wolf eats 10 to 20 pounds (4 to 9 kilograms) of meat. If there is any left, the wolves may come back later.

Before babies are born, a mother and father wolf either dig a new den, enlarge an old fox den, or use a beaver lodge. Often, especially if food is scarce, only the male and female leaders of a pack mate and bear young. A wolf den may be 15 feet (4.5 meters) long and must be high enough for a wolf to stand in. Wolf babies are born in the spring, underground in dens like this one in Alaska.

A group of baby wolves born at the same time to one mother is called a litter. This litter has three pups, but some have ten or more. These pups are only about one week old. They have fine, dark, fuzzy hair, floppy ears, and blunt noses. They look much like dog puppies. Wolf pups cannot see at birth. Each of them weighs only about one pound (half a kilogram). For the first few weeks of their lives, wolf pups nurse—their only food is the milk they get from their mothers. The mother stays close to the pups, making sure they are well fed, clean, and protected. She usually doesn't have to hunt for food herself because the father and other members of the pack bring food to her.

About two weeks after they are born, wolf pups open their eyes and begin to walk. At about three weeks they come out of their den and begin to play outside. Though they still nurse, they start to eat meat. All the members of the pack help care for the pups, bringing food to them. The pups rush up when a wolf returns from hunting. They wag their tails and whine and lick the adult's jaws. The wolf then brings up some of the food it has swallowed and gives it to the pups.

The pups grow very fast, and after about a month they start fighting and tumbling around with each other. After a while they begin to develop a dominance order among themselves. During a fight, one of the pups will roll over on its back to show that it gives up. The other raises its tail to show dominance. Pups also play at hunting by attacking each other, insects, and small animals. These games help pups practice hunting skills they will need when they grow up.

During the summer the pups begin to look like adult wolves, but they stay together in a safe place while the adults hunt. By fall the young wolves join the rest of the pack when it travels. They may join a hunt to help run down prey, but the older wolves make the kill. By winter the young are nearly grown. When they are about two years old, some will stay with the pack while others will leave to find mates and start new packs.

Two hundred years ago there were many thousands of wolves across much of the Northern Hemisphere. But wolves have been hunted, trapped, and poisoned, and only small numbers can still be found in eastern Europe, China, and parts of North America.

Henry David Thoreau, an American naturalist, once wrote, "In wilderness is the preservation of the world." In 1995, conservationists reintroduced wolves into Yellowstone National Park in Wyoming. Some people saw this as a threat to their livestock and even to themselves. After being absent from the park for nearly 70 years, wolves are thriving again where they roamed free in the past. The fate of the wolf is up to us and our continued willingness to share the earth with wild animals.

Smithsonian Mission Statement

For more than 160 years, the Smithsonian has remained true to its mission, "the increase and diffusion of knowledge." Today the Smithsonian is not only the world's largest provider of museum experiences supported by authoritative scholarship in science, history, and the arts but also an international leader in scientific research and exploration. The Smithsonian offers the world a picture of America, and America a picture of the world.

This book is dedicated with love to my first grandchild,
Joel Fauteux Simon.

PHOTO CREDITS: pp. 2–3, 8, 13: © Tom & Pat Leeson; pp. 4, 30: © Alan & Sandy Carey; pp. 7, 32: © Lynn M. Stone; p. 11 © Bob Winsett/Tom Stack and Associates; pp. 14, 17, 21, 22: © Joe McDonald; p. 18 © Thomas Kitchin/Tom Stack and Associates; p. 25: © Rolf Peterson; pp. 26, 29: © Art Wolfe.

The name of the Smithsonian, Smithsonian Institution and the sunburst logo
are registered trademarks of the Smithsonian Institution.
Collins is an imprint of HarperCollins Publishers.

Library of Congress Cataloging-in-Publication Data
Simon, Seymour.
    Wolves / Seymour Simon.
        p.   cm.
    Summary: Text and photographs present the physical characteristics, habits, and natural environment of wolves.
    ISBN 978-0-06-162658-6 (trade bdg.) — ISBN 978-0-06-162657-9 (pbk.)
    1. Wolves—Juvenile literature.   [1. Wolves]   I. Title
QL737.C22S56 1993   92-25924
599.74′442—dc20   CIP
                                                                                         AC

1 2 3 4 5 6 7 8 9 10
❖
Updated Edition